COMPOSTING

All the Skills and Tools You Need to Get Started

(The Complete Guide to Composting and Creating Your Own Compost)

William Davis

Published By William Davis

William Davis

All Rights Reserved

Composting: All the Skills and Tools You Need to Get Started (The Complete Guide to Composting and Creating Your Own Compost)

ISBN 978-1-77485-394-8

All rights reserved. No part of this guide may be reproduced in any form without permission in writing from the publisher except in the case of brief quotations embodied in critical articles or reviews.

Legal & Disclaimer

The information contained in this book is not designed to replace or take the place of any form of medicine or professional medical advice. The information in this book has been provided for educational and entertainment purposes only.

The information contained in this book has been compiled from sources deemed reliable, and it is accurate to the best of the Author's knowledge; however, the Author cannot guarantee its accuracy and validity and cannot be held liable for any errors or omissions. Changes are periodically made to this book. You must consult your doctor or get professional medical advice before using any of the suggested remedies, techniques, or information in this book.

Upon using the information contained in this book, you agree to hold harmless the Author from and against any damages, costs, and expenses, including any legal fees potentially resulting from the application of any of the information provided by this guide. This disclaimer applies to any damages or injury caused by the use and application, whether directly or indirectly, of any advice or information presented, whether for breach of contract, tort, negligence, personal injury, criminal intent, or under any other cause of action.

You agree to accept all risks of using the information presented inside this book. You need to consult a professional medical practitioner in order to ensure you are both able and healthy enough to participate in this program.

TABLE OF CONTENTS

INTRODUCTION 1

CHAPTER 1: COMPOST BASICS 3

CHAPTER 2: COMPOSTING BASICS 19

CHAPTER 3: DIFFERENT TYPES OF COMPOSTING 45

CHAPTER 4: HOW DO I EFFECTIVELY COMPOST? 73

CHAPTER 5: COMPOSING OVER GROUND OR UNDER THE GROUND 80

CHAPTER 6: WHEN TO BEGIN COMPOSTING 107

CHAPTER 7: THE BASICS OF COMPOSTING 121

CHAPTER 8: MAKING A COMPOST HEAP 142

CHAPTER 9: SIMPLE COMPOST CREATION PROCESS 168

CONCLUSION 183

Introduction

Are you aware of many legitimate advantages to composting? Let me begin by saying that it improves the soil it saves money, minimizes the impact you have on the environment and conserves resources!

Whatever your goals the process of composting can be an excellent option for everyone who is interested in it. It's beneficial for you as well as your family's health and is a huge benefit to the ecological environment.

It's been proven that the addition of mulch to the garden can not just improve the soil's fertility but gives your soil various microorganisms as well as nutrients that boost the growth of your plants.

In addition, you must be aware that chemical fertilizers, on the other hand, provide quick access to only a small amount of nutrients. Compost is also beneficial for drainage, improves soil stability, and aids in helping keep moisture in the soil.

Chapter 1: Compost Basics

What exactly is compost?

Compost is a hefty and dark soil-like material that has a slight sweet scent. It is an natural fertilizer and adds nutrients to soil. It is the product of the breakdown and decomposition of a broad variety of organic substances. Composting, which is the process of creating compost, is the process of speeding this process with the proper proportions of materials and careful monitoring (e.g. mixing the material, adding water and protection from rain, etc.) to ensure that, instead of waiting for Mother Nature to decompose these substances, we can do this faster and gain from the final product.

What are the advantages of compost?

Compost is an amazing material for helping your soil and plants. It offers many advantages, including:

Structure of the soil: If one of the fortunate people with an ideal garden with perfect soil, the chances are that your soil isn't ideal. It could be too heavy, which tends to hold on to water, or it could be too sandy and light. Whatever the soil type, composting can help improve the soil's structure for sandy soils, it assists in retaining moisture, while heavier soils benefit from being broken up by compost.

Increases the nutrients in your soil: As you plant your crops your soil is empty of the nutrients. To ensure that your soil is in top shape, a mixture of fertilizers should be utilized to fill your soil. This isn't an easy (and costly) job. Compost however is a fantastic source of all the necessary of nutrients that replenish.

Introduces beneficial organisms to the soil. Compost is made by the work of a myriad of fungi, bacteria and soil-based organisms. They are then added to the soil in conjunction in the form of compost. They continue to help plant growth by dissolving the material as well as allowing for greater accessibility and absorption of nutrients.

The benefit of a balanced, year-round fertilizer is that one negative aspect of fertilizers is that according to what you're growing , they must be used at specific periods in the growth cycle and care should be used when adding your fertilizerto ensure that you do not end up burning or damaging your plant. Compost however does not have any of the issues attached to it. It is a complete variety of nutrientsavailable, you do not need to worry about making too much of it or adding it in the season of growth or outside of season. It is truly the key ingredient that makes any garden flourish!

It reduces the amount of waste that is generated: A huge variety of materials can be utilized to create compost. The majority of this material will go straight into your garbage and eventually to the landfill which is where methane, a greenhouse gas, is created. It is estimated that around 30% of household waste can be diverted from trash pile to the compost heap.

What is the process of making compost?

Compost is produced by the natural decomposition of the material by a range of fungi, bacteria, and other living organisms. This process can occur when oxygen is present (termed aerobic) or without oxygen (anaerobic). When oxygen is present, the rate of decomposition is very quick (relatively in terms of speed) However, in the event that there's not enough oxygen like at the bottom of a filled waste pile Anaerobic breakdown is likely to take place. This is a slower process (though decomposition will take place and compost will be formed) with various bacteria in the environment. Anaerobic decomposition results in an unpleasant smelly compost pile. Although the organisms are able to break down almost all materials but the rate at which it breaks down will depend on the size of the initial materials, with the smaller pieces decomposing faster than larger ones. This is because when the material is cut into smaller fragments e.g. an apple cut up in blenders There is more surface area for bacteria to develop as opposed to when the carrot is intact.

In order to compost, there are nine components required. These include:

The Nitrogen/Green Material is in essence that the material in green is a material that is rich in nitrogen. It acts as a contact-paper that activates the decomposition process that produces heat. When you look around, there are many green materials which can be used to create compost. This includes grass cuttings vegetables and fruits, scraps of vegetable and fruit and tea bags, waste coffee grounds, tea bags, etc. A more extensive list can be found in the section 3.

Carbon/Brown Material - The brown material is rich in Carbon. This is the food source for diverse microorganisms that live that are found in your compost. There are many sources of brown material to add to your compost pile, including fallen leaves and cardboard, sawdust, flowering plants straw. Although both brown and green substances are needed to make compost, it's important not to fill your compost pile by putting excessive amounts of one as well as the opposite. The proportion of each is discussed in section 5. The brown material can also act in a different way to aid the composting process. They can also serve to bulk up the compost in order to keep the pile porosity which allows for air flow.

Compost is made of oxygen by an increase in microorganisms taking in green and brown material, creating compost as a result from this process. This decomposition process is the most effective when aerobic, also known as oxygen-loving bacteria are present. While fungi and bacteria are able to develop in the absence of oxygen, a distinct set of organisms are at play (anaerobic kinds).

Anaerobic growth results in the slowing of decomposition, the matting of the materials within and the creation of odours that smell foul. Once the bacteria have consumed oxygen aerobic digestion ceases and the bacteria will begin to die with an increase in temperature within the heap. This is why it is essential to allow air into your compost pile. There is no fancy equipment required to accomplish this, just use a fork or rake to rotate your compost pile every now and then.

Water - fungi and bacteria require water for growth which is why it is crucial to ensure that the right amount of moisture is maintained in your compost pile. If it becomes too dry, the process of decomposition will slow down and the compost pile could attract small rodents and vermin If it happens to be too moist it can lead to the material to clump, making it anaerobic. The right amount of water can be judged by rubbing it with your fingertips - basically, it should feel like an old towel or sponge which has been squeezed out ("damp yet dry but not moist"). The moisture can be added by the green material you mix in (your vegetables leftovers) or you can add it yourself with watering cans or hoses. In addition, depending on how your compost is constructed, it could be exposed to the elements. If it is, then you'll need to give your compost heap some protection from rain e.g. by covering it with Tarpaulin, so that it is not getting wet.

Fragment Size - the dimension of the material that you place into your compost pile will have an important impact on the amount of time the composting will take. The bigger the pile, the greater the decompositionprocess, the more time it will take to make your compost. Bacteria live on the material. If something is cut down to a smaller size it will have a larger surface area, and will give more space for fungi and bacteria to thrive on. It doesn't mean that you have to cut everything into pieces before you put in however breaking things down as much as you can is certainly beneficial.

Dimensions of Compost Pile or Compost Bin The dimensions of your compost bin or compost pile the size you pick will be dependent on your requirements and the the size that your yard. The most common rule is to not make your pile too big. It is important for the bugs to begin to grow and decay and generate heat inside the heap (making them warm and warm contact on the outside) which assists in decomposition. A one that's not large is a challenge for heat to be produced within the pile, which results in decomposition zones within the pile. Likewise, the one that is too small could result in the heat being scattered to the outside, but not retaining the heat inside the pile, thereby slowing down the process of decomposition. It is recommended that your pile is at minimum 7/8 cubic feet (approximately 2 feet long, 2 feet wide, and 2 feet high) and not more than 27 cubic yards (3 feet long, 3 feet wide, 3 feet high)

Temperature - as explained earlier, during decomposition at its peak, the temperature inside of the pile could go up to 140oF (60oC). (Note that temperatures of the compost pile will change as decomposition takes place and ranges between 60oF (15oC) up to 140oF (60oC) Decomposition will be more rapid at greater temperatures) This is ideal to ensure a quick and efficient decomposition. The best compost pile should remain at the temperature of this, but due to the external weather conditions it may not always be feasible. To prevent your compost pile from becoming too hot, you might want to think about placing the compost container in a semi shaded area of your garden, and not necessarily in full sunlight. In winter, you might be able to add insulation for your compost pile to keep heat in. Many have used Styrofoam insulation on edges of their compost pile or black tarpaulin at the top of their pile to accomplish this aim. Be sure to take care used to ensure that when the insulation, it doesn't hinder the ventilation in the heap.

Placement - Your compost pile must be situated in a cool space, but not in an area that receives direct sunlight or that is exposed to too much winds. Although air and heat are vital components of decomposition direct sunlight and winds can cause drying from the compost heap.

Microorganisms: We could spend time putting together our compost piles with the correct proportions of browns and greens as well as ensuring that there's enough moisture however, without microorganisms that break down the material and wait for quite a while for the compost to be finished. In order to make compost, a wide variety of organisms are required to complete the various stages of breakdown. What is the source of this massive and complex collection of microorganisms? In fact, as my science teacher used to tell me "microbes can be found all over the place!" There will be plenty of bugs floating around as well as on the soil that we put in the compost to kick things off. To lend an extra helping hand I would suggest putting your compost on the soil, and letting it be in contact with the soil. I will also include one or two spades of soil to my mix because it contains all the bugs that are needed to speed up the process of decomposition. There are starter cultures available for purchase however, if you want to do not spend your hard-earned cash, just a tiny bit of soil is all you need.

Chapter 2: Composting Basics

Composting Garden

The best location to place your compost is crucial. In general, it is best not to put your compost stack or compartment in a location susceptible to massive fluctuations in dampness and temperature. This is due to the fact that the microorganisms which transform organic materials into compost are inclined towards regular conditions.

Selecting a garden location with adequate shade can prevent it from drying out during bright days, or getting wet in rainy weather. It is also possible to put the compost pile on top of the soil directly.

It may seem appealing to set your container or stack on sections for clearing however, it is essential that the material is accessible to worms insects, and soil-loving microorganisms that are a part of it.

when it comes to causing food waste to decay and decay, placing them directly on the ground will result in a more favorable and better outcome.

Techniques

Everyone has their own needs, and at a moment in time, at a minimum one of these methods might fit your day-to-day conditions, and you could eventually alter the way you regularly compost over the course of your life. They all function in varying amounts for different reasons Certain are more effective than others while others are essentially distinctive.

* Open Air Composting (Hot Composting)

The composting method is usually a heap of brown and green material that is located inside your garden. It is usually built as a large container comprised of whatever you find compact and simple to build. However, it could be constructed using bins, a few that are flipped on their sides. Wire

The confines can also be constructed using funnels around their edges to hold the heat and hold in water. Anything that has to do with sustainability in relation to hot water systems could be addressed. Open-air composting can be generally thought of as an approach to composting hot.

*Direct Composting (In-ground Composting)

Direct compost is the process of making an open channel or opening within the soil and then covering the remaining materials. It is also the most well-established and efficient method for composting the soil. However, as every other method for composting it has its own limitations. One of them is that it can take quite a while to break down, unless you've got material that is all chopped into pieces. However, it does create a wealth of worms that will help to maintain your garden and also improve the soil.

* Tumbler Composting (Hot composting)

It comes in a variety of shapes and sizes , from single-to-twofold units that can be purchased in bulk quantities at your local home store. It is common to require 2 of them, so you can let one be in storage for a few months before it breaks down and it's emptied. When the process of decomposition is complete it is time to top the second one up. This could be a great solution if the brown and green wastes are abundant and you have enough room for the system to be placed.

*Composting from Worm Farms (Vermicomposting)

Composting using Worms For a large number of people is the most widely known and utilized method of composting, in light of their capacity to protect worms, cultivate them as well as make compost and stop rats from entering the composting area. Castings made by worms have concentrated nutrients that have low nitrogen content, in contrast with other composting strategies. Worm farms can be utilized regardless of having gardens or no nursery.

* EMO Composting (Bacteria Composting)

Its EMO (Effective microorganisms) composting system is utilized to primarily compost indoors and is a great option for anyone who appreciates this method. The most popular product that makes use of EMO's is Bokashi but other models can benefit from the technique, and, in addition there are other systems that use carbon channels on the cover to remove all kinds of unpleasant odours. There is also the possibility of making use of both of these systems. This can be done in situations that one of them is in use while the other one is being filled.

*Combination Composting (Compot Composting)

This type of technique, also referred to as Compot composting, is an amalgamation method.

that involves direct composting such as worm or vemicomposting open-air composting, open-air EMO composting. Each of the components of composting are utilized and can be used in a variety of conditions.

* Commercial Composting

Commercial composting is different from backyard composting, and uses different types of materials. The compost is made in rows that are long using materials such as sawdust pine bark, ferrous sulphate and perhaps ammonia sulfate in some form mixed together. Compost is worked in the space of 3 to 4 days and mostly completed in about one month and a quarter for packing. There aren't many nutrients found in compost that's produced commercially.

* Mechanical Composting

Mechanical composting is an effective method of composting which makes use of electricity (electricity) to create heat, which helps to rotate the

Content that is required to generate waste in a semi-composed form within a 24-hour period.

Composting Tools

If you're already gardening, chances are you'll be able to leap straight into composting using the tools that are close to you. If you're just beginning in the process of planting and composting you'll be pleased to know that the cost on the tools you need.

* Gloves

Gloves that fit perfectly and are extremely comfortable and are vital for your gardening and composting activities. If they're not feeling comfortable while you're doing your tasks, you're likely going to remove them and throw them away and forget the place you put them which could leave you with burns and scratches.

* Safety Glasses

If you cut compost materials using shredding machines or chipper, or even using a hand tool that is used to cleave, you should wear eye protection glasses and safety goggles in order to shield your eyes from potentially dangerous UFOs (unidentified flying organics). Make sure you wear these glasses while handling large amounts of thin, prickly, or thin stems that might fly away in a random manner and strike you in the eye.

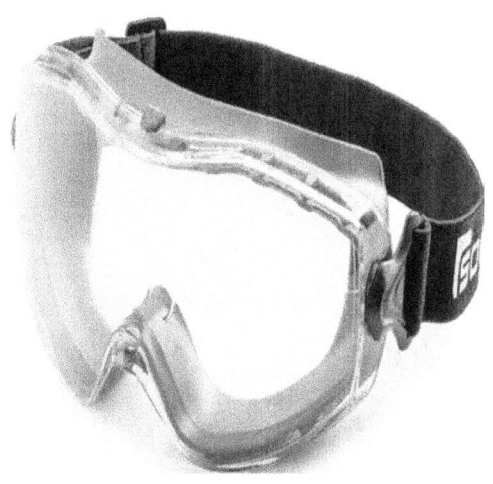

Pitch and Compost Fork

The forks have the length of four or five thin and tapered upward-curving prongs. The design is constructed in the manner that it's easy to slide down into a mass of organic matter, allowing the user to move and carry the material to another location. Additionally, they're ideal for moving large quantities of heavy, bulky organic matter such as straw, feed leaves, straw, and other trimmings of plants. Use them for creating compost piles mixing and then turning them over until they're well decomposed.

* Digging Fork

Also known as a burrowing fork or spading fork. This tool features flattened prongs, which have shorter lengths, and whose

have a thickness that is greater than that for the pitchfork. This fork is helpful in mixing compost and turning it into a form that's nearly ready to go or in digging massive and fully-finished compost from the heap before blending it into gardens.

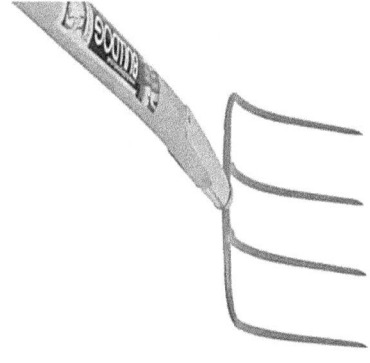

*Shovels and Spades

Both words are used frequently and often interchanged, but the wording can vary by the area. The shovel is a tool that is designed for the transfer of material with a lip that is raised to the edges that form the edge. A shovel is different from a spade.

since it has a straight head, with sharp edges and can be employed to dig.

* Hose

When composting, a reliable water supply is vital. A high amount of moisture is a important element of compost that is being created and is necessary to soak the material in composting.

at times, allowing it to let it decompose properly.

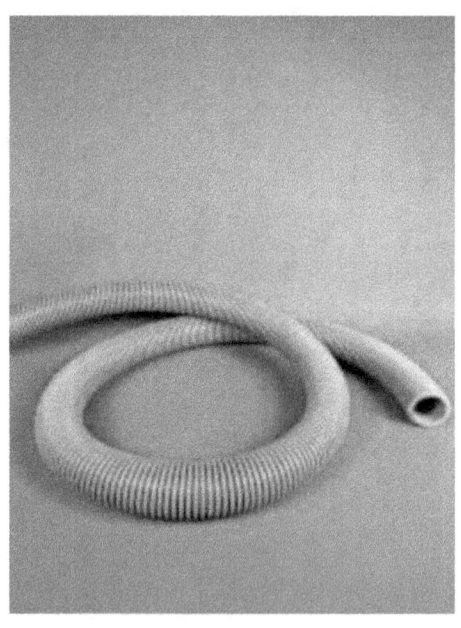

* Tarps or Buckets

The process of transporting compost from one location to another, within your garden, is cheap and simple as using a heavy plastic bucket, though not always a light family one or a cover. A bucket is

extremely useful in moving small amounts of compost. It is very useful for moving small amounts of.

* Compost Thermometer

An compost thermometer connected to a probe that is long at the end of it, approximately 20 inches or 0.5m. The thermometer is placed in the middle of the

compost pile to keep track of and monitor the temperature.

What is the best way to compost your food at home?

Composting can be made using any kind of vegetable or fruit piece along with their cores and peels. Home appliances could also be used. In some cases, it is recommended to eliminate seeds since they could begin sprouting if they're not completely decayed or broken.

Here are some food items or items that can be composted:

* Scraps of vegetables and fruits

* Eggshells (lightly crushed)

* Grounds and coffee filters

* Newspapers

* Cardboard

* Nutshells

* Houseplants

* Teabag

* Sawdust

* Cotton Rag

* Fire ashes

* Vacuum and dryer cleaners dust

* Pet hide and hair

* Wood chips

* Trimming of the yard and grass clippings

What to avoid:

They can also create undesirable smells, attract rodents or cause the creation of compost that can be harmful to be used in food gardens.

* Dairy products

* Fats, oils, grease

* Fish bones, meat or meat or scraps of fish or meat.

* Weeds

* Eggs

* Yard trimmings that have been treated with pesticides

* Pet waste

* Twigs and leaves of the black walnut trees

* Plants with diseases

* Charcoal or coal Ash

Learning about the carbon-nitrogen ratio

Organisms involved in decomposing require carbon energy as well as nitrogen for growth The composter should strive to supply both in the appropriate proportion required by microorganisms. The ideal ratio of C/N for composting lies somewhere between 25:1 to 30:1, with carbon having the highest percentage. If you have some experiences, you'll be able to get an impression of the best mixtures.

Carbonaceous substances are typically yellow or brown dry, coarse, and massive in comparison with nitrogenous materials which are green, gooey robust and succulent. Materials with a high content of carbon include mainly plant materials such as straw, cornstalks and sawdust and leaves. This is of materials that have

The high nitrogenous content is a by-product of animals, mainly. Making use of the material from animals will not hinder your composting efforts. Other examples of materials that are rich in nitrogen include grass clippings, blood meal or manure from poultry as well as alfalfa meal. Certain items, such as clover garbage from the kitchen and bedding mixed manure offer a wide range of carbon-nitrogen ratios.

The majority or weight of the pile increases by an addition of carbon material and forms organic gums which are thought to be found in large amounts in the humus. Nitrogen is crucial since it assists microorganisms to grow in size by accelerating the process of reproduction rapidly. But, substances with low nitrogen content will degrade within a time period but will not reach the temperature required to create a hot type of composting. If there's excess nitrogen, similar to carbon will be transformed into ammonia, and then lost in a way that is clearly identifiable by its scent. It continues to do this for only some time until

The material is able to settle. If it is a more severe case, the abundance of nitrogen could make the heap swell and anaerobic. This is because it is believed that carbon-rich materials help to improve air circulation.

The Time to Start Composting

When you decide to create compost manure, it is important to be aware that making an excellent compost takes time. It isn't possible to make it in a short time. The length of time that the process really requires is contingent on a variety of factors. Some experts believe that any time from a couple of months or even three years is a sufficient duration.

It will be clear that your compost has been made when it's dark brown, and appears to be abundant soil. Many containers have an opening at the bottom to check. It could smell like earth, but it isn't a bad smell.

The whole process of composting depends on these factors:

* The level of ripening that you require.

* The variety of items that you can put in the canister.

The extent of your commitment is evident by the frequency you move the pile.

* The surface area of the material being used.

* How large it is that the soil has.

* The amount of air circulation and dampness of your bin.

* The purpose that composting bins have.

* Where the bin is.

Chapter 3: Different Types Of Composting

Composting is the process of the breakdown of organic materials. The different kinds of composting are described in the sections below. This includes:

* Piles Composting

* Bin Composting

* Trench Composting

* Anaerobic Composting

* Worm Composting

* Tumbler Composting

Piles Composting

This is among the most efficient ways to decrease the amount of trash your family is able to dump into the landfill. Based on the EPA around 30% of the waste we dispose of is garden and food waste. This reduces not only methane emissions which is a major cause of global warming, however, composting can also help control the odor of waste. What's the most rewarding benefit? A rich fertilizer you can put in the garden or offer to your preferred company.

The selection of a spot in your yard to compost is the most efficient way to compost.

Water is the most important ingredient to decomposition. A dry pile will take longer to break down. Pick a place which is easily accessible using the help of a garden hose. Some people set up the compost pile in a remote part of their garden to ensure that it isn't seen by others and it's difficult to maintain it by watering it. If you have a pile near the greenhouse, think about collecting rainwater from your roof into an insulated rain barrel to water the compost.

All you need to do is construct an area of seven feet, or less the backyard, and then dig an opening. It is important to ensure that your space doesn't exceed 7 meters or else the airflow could cause problems.

All you need to do is mix the ingredients together and then take care of the required ingredients, and your compost is ready in no time. There are almost no other tools or equipment are needed.

Ideally, you should be 5 feet of space. If you regularly add layers make sure you get it each time you add dirt.

A lot of the organisms are ones you'd like to have in a pile are able to escape the soil of your garden. Compost piles set on canvas or concrete pad can be damaged by weeds because they are separated from the soil. If you're concerned about weeds growing out of your lawn, take grass from beneath the pallet, and then place firewood, cardboard or newspapers between the soil and the compost.

Bin Composting

It's a container into the which waste from organic sources is disposed of over time to compost. Certain bins are indefinite that means you can continue adding waste, whereas others are composted using a certain mixture of ingredients are added to the mix at the same time.

The same process will take place as time passes in "heap" and "heap" composting even without casing. However, decomposition could be increased with just one container. It is dependent on the kind that compost containers you pick containers also be beneficial in making it more difficult for rats to reach your compost. There are many kinds of compost bins, some can be purchased at a store, while others are made.

Potential components for making a compost bins include:

* Lumber

* Cinder blocks

* Ceramic

* Wire fencing

* Stone

* Plastic

What can you put into your Compost Bin

* Clippings of grass

* Maximum disease-free garden garbage

* Coffee grounds

* Newspaper in black and white

* Lettuce

* Cardboard

* Potato peels

* Printer paper

* Banana peels

* Vegetable food scraps

* Avocado skins

* Tree leaves

* Vegetarian animal fertilizer (e.g., cows, rabbits, horses, hamsters, etc.)

The bins hold water, heat and will compost faster. However, any open heap can eventually decompose. All compost bins in the shop must be fertilized so long as they're not wet and retaining heat, offering drainage, and removing the air.

Trench Composting

Trench composting is the process of composting garden and kitchen waste, which includes weeds. It require little effort on the part and enriches the soil in only one month. The process of composting is transparent, completely odorless and is able to be utilized almost anywhere within the gardens. The most important thing is that it does doesn't require reverses.

Composting in ditches is easy. Create a pit or trench in any form that is 12 inches deep inside your yard. Add up six inches or more of compost, such food wastes garden plants, small cuts thinned, weeds, and thinning and then bury or dig dirt into the pit.

The best reason to compost in the trenches is that it's extremely easy to compost. It isn't necessary to stress about keeping proper moisture levels and ventilation or sorting, similar to the compost heap.

Trench composting is a great way to save cash as the nutrients they supply help plants to lessen the need for commercial fertilizers and pesticides.

It can be organized or for free using compost if you'd like. There are three different methods you can apply in the garden. They all work and all are founded on the notion that you shouldn't plant directly onto the compost material because this will cause the area to sink when the material begins to decompose.

* Trench Rotation

"Dig and Drop"

* Trenching Between Rows

In soils that are well-drained and humus-rich, in which there are a variety of microorganisms and microorganisms in the soil, the material excava decay within a few months. In soils that are not properly drained it can be a full year or more.

Compost piles are able to accommodate the variety of insects both bad and good. In winter, they're especially attractive to mice and rats. Compost piles typically dry in winter , if they are not watered or turned over which makes them more appealing to tiny artists.

By using this method, you can create a trench approximately 1 meter deep . You will then dig a hole to put your kitchen waste into it. When you combine the waste in a layer and soil, you will also add another layer of soil.

When the trench is at a at a level with the ground, you can use the landing pad and sowing. The major benefit of this method is that it doesn't require an exact procedure.

The drawback is that the area is not functional as long as the trench has not been filled. In the autumn, it is suggested to dig a trench to make it ready for plants in the spring.

Anaerobic Composting

In anaerobic composting, the decomposition occurs because oxygen (O) is absent or is not present. In this way microorganisms in anaerobic environments control and create intermediates, such as methane, hydrogen sulfur sulfide, organic acids, and other substances.

Organic matter is decomposed into oxygen, the principal products are water, heat, as well as carbon dioxide (CO2). Carbon dioxide is definitely one of the most dangerous greenhouse gases that contributes global warming. However, anaerobic degradation creates methane (CH4) which is a more potent greenhouse gas.

The product that comes out of methane is the result of anaerobic digestion, that can be used to heat, generate electricity and cooking. Anaerobic refers to a state where oxygen is extremely restricted.

Aerobic respiration is quicker than anaerobic because bacteria are metabolized more quickly by heat and oxygen.

The results of anaerobic composition include carbon dioxide and methane.

Anaerobic digestion techniques capture methane and allow us to make use of methane for our benefit. Methane capture is essential since methane is the most dominant greenhouse gas that is a result of changes in the climate in the atmosphere, when released.

Anaerobic composting is an additional relatively simple and efficient composting technique that is simple and convenient.

All you need be doing is to fill your trash bags with the proper elements, then secure them and put the bags in an arid location in your backyard for six months. You can open your bag after six months, and you will have compost ready for utilize.

Additionally, you can utilize compost containers to aid in anaerobic composting.

One of the biggest environmental benefits of anaerobic digestion is its ability to reduce the emission of greenhouse gases. DA functions can replace the energy consumed from fossil fuels through the capture of methane gas that is released to the atmosphere.

Anaerobic digestion however does not require oxygen. Instead, the components are kept in a sealed container - the bacteria reside within the organic material. This process is slower than conventional composting, however the outcome is more effective. As the material decomposes Anaerobically methane, an important component of biogas, escapes.

Worm Composting

Growing worms can be expensive or cost-effective. If you have a bit of imagination and a little savvy it is possible to make the things you have in your home which are adequate to start. The only expense is red worms. However, when you obtain fertilizer, you can get red worms that have been rotten in manure that you can use to feed the farm.

They are red worms that are related to the ones found in manure or in compost. They differ from normal earthworms, and excel in converting organic waste into extremely beneficial fertilizers.

It is necessary to have bedding and food for the worms. These will be described in the next chapters. However, these are the newspaper and kitchen scraps. There is no need to spend money, since you have the ability to get access to a large number of newspapers for free.

All you require is something to keep the worms. You can purchase worm growth kits with containers, or create your own it's easy. All you need is a box that can be molded and lid. It must be of a standard size. However, you can get plastic drawer lids at stores that sell discount items for a few dollars and they'll work well.

Additionally, an old refrigerator can be used to create a healthy soil for worms that you can get at no cost. Lay it out upon its side, pull out drawers and containers, and then hold the gate open by using a piece of wood so that it's almost an inch. This will create an air flow which the worms will love. If you need to, drill several holes into the rear of the worm to drain any excess fluid. In warmer regions refrigerators protect your worms from warmth and keeps them warm in winter. In regions that are colder, ensure that your worms are warm. This could mean you might need to relocate them to a sheltered area, or garaging them or insulate them.

The majority of worm buckets can be found in dark-colored greens or even blacks as the worms do not like sunlight direct. If you purchase an opaque plastic container, put a lid on the outside to keep the container from opening. Be aware that worms are undercover creatures and are not able to be able to escape from the edges of the worm's body to consume the food items.

This is pretty much all you need to start a farm of worms, and as you'll see that it's not going to cost you an enormous amount of cash. The benefit of growing Worms is that it's an excellent way to make lots of fertilizer at a low cost and also recycle kitchen waste in a natural way.

Vermicomposting or composting worms is among the most efficient methods and creates the most fertile soil.

For composting worm, you need:

* Red Worms

* Tiger Worms

However, you won't likely to see them in your backyard however, you might have to purchase the worms. Earthworms eat garbage and transform it into quality compost.

Composting worms are extremely efficient and can be time-consuming. Make sure to provide your worms with appropriate food to allow the manure in order to keep it healthy.

It is possible to use plastic containers like cages, cages or crates to keep the worms. Be sure the worm cages can be properly cleaned as otherwise, the worms may drown in the moisture that is collected from food waste or vegetable skins.

The worm containers must be treated at temperatures of 55-75°C.

Tumbler Composting

It is an enclosed bin that is able to rotate to mix compost.

Compost bowls were designed to make composting more efficient and more quickly. Composters that rotate aren't like compost bins. Compost containers are made to sit on the ground and the majority of compost bins come with an open bottom.

A quality tumble dryer makes turning effortless. If you want to quickly grease and finish the job correctly then you could use a normal compost bucket or pile when the compost is accessible to be turned over. It's significantly less costly and offers more exercise options.

What is compost?

* Asterixes from the fire.

* Dung from herbivores that comes from animals

* Paper towels

* Cardboard rolls brown paper bags cereal boxes

* Coffee grounds and filters

* Clean paper

* Wool and cotton rugs

* Crushed eggshells

* Hay & straw

* Dryer & vacuum cleaner lint

* Hair & fur

* Nutshells

* Houseplants

* Leaves

* Seaweed

* Fruits & vegetables

* Tea bags and tea

* Newspaper shreds

* Yard trimmings and grass clippings

* Wood chips, toothpicks, sawdust, burnt matches

What is not to be Compost

* Meat, eggs, fish or poultry scraps

* Charcoal Ash or coal

* Dairy products

* Insect-ridden plants or diseases

* The twigs of a black walnut tree or leaves

* Lard, fats grease, oils, or fats

* Pet waste

* Garden trimmings that are treated by pesticides

Chapter 4: How Do I Effectively Compost?

Your compost needs appropriate monitoring and care to ensure your compost to be properly decomposed. The best practices for compost production can be a lengthy process, however there are numerous strategies you can employ to your composting to make decomposition more efficient and more efficient. Here are some strategies that you can follow to compost your garden The following are some of them:

Location

The ideal location for the compost heap is outdoors in direct sunlight. The sun's rays dry the compost pile and direct exposure to the high winds will ensure that it is keep the compost pile cool and dry. It is also possible to put the pile in soil that has drainage systems that are well-designed to keep moisture from getting too high. Make sure to not place your pile on top of a wooden structure or tree since it gets in contact with compost can cause decay. It is also possible to include additional considerations, such as to keep your pile out of garden activities and lawns close to water sources, or in areas that have enough space to store temporary organic waste.

Volume

The size that you compost your waste is important for good growth and development of the microorganisms in your compost. Your compost pile must be big enough to hold the heat, but smaller enough to allow air to get to the middle. The minimum significant size of your compost pile is 3X3X3 inches and must not exceed the permitted limit of 5ftX5ft at any length. If your compost pile is less than 1 cubic yard then you must protect the sides. If your pile is higher than 5 feet in height and you have to turn the pile frequently to increase air flow and prevent anaerobic activities.

Pile Construction

The most efficient way to build a compost heap is to add the composting materials in a series when they are available. If you wish to make your compost to be more efficient and have sufficient greens and browns, you can make it by layering two kinds of compost in roughly 4-6 inches increments. Continue mixing the layers as you add materials. The batch pile will compost faster than the standard kind of pile. If you don't have a lot of compostable material, you can layer the material you've added as more material becomes available. This technique is more laborious than batch pile but it's the most frequent method utilized by smaller households.

Maintenance of the Pile

Maintaining the compost heap is an essential aspect of compost gardening. The amount of maintenance required completely dependent on the person However, turning the compost pile at least once each week is recommended. Most people perform the adding and turning work in tandem which allows the new material to be incorporated quicker. Sometimes, adding water is needed, however turning the pile is enough to allow the moisture to be distributed more evenly.

If the five elements which are discussed in the previous part of the book considered while maintaining the pile, the finished compost will be produced fairly quickly. The compost pile is complete when it cools down to 10 degrees F. at ambient temperature, and shrinks to about 1/3 of the volume of your pile. Your compost must be dark with a pleasant smell and with no visible remains of decomposed materials.

Pest Avoidance

Pests aren't good for your compost pile, and it is important to stay clear of any compost material that can attract rodents and pests like fish and meat scraps bone cheeses, butter, and dairy and meat products. Bread and other foods that contain high levels of sugar and carbohydrates can attract pests, so try to avoid these in any way you can. If your region is plagued by rodents or pests, you should consider purchasing commercial containers to your pile of compost. This will keep the rodents from getting to it. It is recommended to cover your pile with completed compost or carbonated material like straw could aid in the control of pests.

Health Concerns

It is important to be aware of health concerns while making the compost. It is advisable to clean your hands after you have worked to prevent any illness. The normal allergic reaction can occur occasionally because of the presence of fungi and mold in compost. If you're suffering from an allergy of any kind wear a dust mark throughout the composting process as well as maintenance, and when rotating the pile.

Chapter 5: Composing Over Ground Or Under The Ground

How to Build an Organic Compost Pile that is above the the ground

It's not hard to create a compost heap above the ground. You do not require a huge space. In order to reach the ideal temperature is a major aim, you'll need to ensure that your compost pile isn't less than 3 feet in width and three feet high, and three feet in length. The golden rule of three feet must be followed until later. The 3 foot (about 1 cubic yard) is the minimum amount that will provide the ideal temperature to eliminate harmful microbes and clear of weeds. But that doesn't necessarily mean smaller piles won't not achieve the desired objectives.

The difference is that larger piles are more likely to work due to their size which makes the temperature rise. However, anything greater than 8 feet isn't optimal. If compost piles are too large, they run the possibility of fire. Another disadvantage of having a huge compost piles is that big compost piles can be difficult to aerate properly.

If you're planning on making a compost heap, first you need to clear the area of ground. It is necessary to choose a location slightly away from trees or rapidly growing vines. You don't want to be in a place in which the root of those plants could be able to penetrate the compost and take away the nutrients. Additionally, you must remove any seeds or weeds that are present on the area. This is essential in case the compost doesn't get sufficiently hot that the seeds can grow in the event that the compost is used for fertilizer or pot soil. The ideal place for your compost piles should be able to drain and be slightly higher. Additionally, ensure the compost heaps you have are away from homes silos, gardens, or even gardens because the piles are a magnet for insects.

When you build large piles, ensure that footpaths are laid at intervals of 8 feet. This is essential to ensure an easy flow of wheels. It is then possible to line the area around it with a plastic liner to avoid getting root intrusion. If you're concerned about moles or other animals that burrow within your area it is possible to apply a layer of hardware cloth to guard against the dangers. Do not place the pile on top of the fence of a wooden one. Compost materials may cause wood to stain and can also encourage it to degrade.

If you've found a suitable place to build your compost then the next step is to break up the components into smaller pieces. Don't forget to save some sticks around to help create foundations. As was mentioned previously, keep in mind that the bigger the area of your composting ingredients, the more quickly the process of breaking them down. To begin you'll require an organic waste layer. Make sure you leave enough space in the base of your compost to facilitate drainage and create an airflow chimney.

It is recommended to create layers of green and brown debris. Utilizing sticks and split logs is strongly encouraged as they assist in keeping everything together and provide support. Since the middle of the compost is where weights are supported most, the largest sticks are recommended for the space. However, the structure isn't crucial if you move your pile every time. So, you can use an electric wood chipper in order to obtain the most surface area that will result in the most rapid decomposition.

If you are putting more green waste in your compost heap, be sure to place fresh waste at the bottom or near thorns. It is necessary to put up a barrier like this to keep Raccoons and skunks off. However, pests will traverse small spaces and snakes are attracted by them. This is why you should make sure to wear a protective garment prior to turning your pile.

Don't put off building your pile until you've run out of materials. It is recommended to use tiny layers of materials in the green color approximately 4 inches in thickness. However the most dense layer of brown material is 7-inches thick. If green waste isn't readily available, you may use manure from sheep, cow goat, or another grass eater. The droppings of dogs and cats could contain a variety of disease-causing agents. So, avoid using as a substitute for green waste. Horse dung is also not healthy because they generally contain a lot of grass seeds.

If snow or rain appears excessively heavy in your region it is recommended to put a blanket over the pile using an cover. Insufficient moisture doesn't slow the process of decomposition. We've covered how to tell if there's excessive moisture in the previous chapter. It is recommended to avoid excessive moisture. To shield your compost from weather extremes it is recommended to utilize dead trees, or keep your compost in a building that is not being used. Once you've completed the steps essential, wait patiently and let nature do the rest.

Digging a hole to create an underground

If you do not have the space to compost on the ground, you can actually make it underground. You can compost underground using two pits. It should be 2 yards, 2 feet wide, and 3 feet long, and to the depth that is 2 feet. Set up cement blocks around the edges, leaving one side to remain open. The hole can be covered by putting a wooden lid that rests on the block that is about 8 inches in height. After that, your underground pit is now ready for composting.

If you are putting garbage in the hole, put a layer of dirt approximately 4 inches thick over it. Then, remove from the container and stir the heap using a spading fork. It is unlikely encounter issues with animals digging in the pit. If you require additional composting, the only thing you have to do is expand the size of your pit.

Compost Containers for Compost

Compost containers are crucial because they store the important compost materials that can be used in agriculture. The compost container can be handled believing that you are doing your best to protect the environmental. But, a lack of understanding the proper way to handle it will do damage that is more harmful than beneficial.

The first step is be aware that there are many things which can be disposed of in compost bins, however, there are some things that shouldn't go into. Each composting technique aims to create high-quality materials that are rich in a mix of browns and greens i.e. substances that are high in Nitrogen and Carbon. This mixture allows for adequate amounts of earthworms and bacteria that can add fertilizers to your soil and enhance the soil's texture.

It is essential to make sure that items with acidic content like citrus fruits do not go in compost bins. These substances can destroy bacteria and other beneficial microorganisms vital to breakdown organic matter. It is also recommended to not put specific plants in compost bins. For instance, weeds that contain seeds are not an ideal addition to your compost heap. There might not be enough heat to eliminate the seeds. So, your garden could end up in a mess sooner than you anticipated.

There are commercially-available compost bins that assist in keeping your compost in a neat and contained. Make sure that the containers you purchase aren't too costly. If not, you can make your own plastic container. Plastic compost containers are a great way to provide insulation and warmth essential to accelerate the process of decomposition. The majority of the containers sold are made of recycled plastics. The products made from recycled compost are highly recommended since they can help reduce environmental pollution and help make our planet a better one to inhabit.

Making Your Choices About the Composting Materials You Want to Use

Dry Leaves

Utilizing dry leaves as a compost material is a wonderful idea. There is a widespread complaint that leaves with no moisture don't break down. If you're experiencing this issue, we'll talk about some ways to help you succeed by the composting of dry leaves.

The first step is to include extra Nitrogen to dry leaves. The most effective Nitrogen supplement that can help reduce the breakdown of dry leaves compost quickly is manure. The suggested mix should comprise of five parts dry leaves compost and 1 part of manure. If manure is not available Other Nitrogen supplements such as cotton seed meal dried blood, bone meal are known to be effective alternatives. Compost heaps generally begin getting hot due to the presence of Nitrogen and provide the right material for bacteria to work on. Additionally, you can include 2 cups blood that has been dried to each wheelbarrow of leaves that are dry.

Another way to improve the dry leaf composting is to crush the leaves. Don't be shocked! It's a fantastic method to make the process of decomposition considerably easier. It's enjoyable working on a compost pile that is composed of shredded materials because of the easy handling. Don't forget to turn the pile at least once every three days. It's not hard to turn a pile of dry or shredded leaves. It is, after all, soft and airy! If it is necessary you would like to wrap the heap in an afghan of plastic. This will prevent the heap from becoming extremely warm or dry, however it will also help keep the warmth within it.

Woody Plant Trimmings

If you don't want to cook the waste, you can simply compost plant trimmings made of wood like stems, twigs, and smaller branches. However stumps, big branches and tree trunks aren't as suitable for composting. But, you can make log piles that will eventually decay to produce excellent compost.

If a small amount of woody trimmings and other slim substances are also involved it is possible to transfer them to the compost bin. They will, in fact, decay much faster than you'd ever imagine. But, if the amounts are excessive it is better off using shredders instead. Shredders are a great option to remove woody stems that are not more than 3-4 centimeters in diameter. Then, you can use the fragments to make heaps compost to be used in the future. Milling is usually a way to accelerate the process of decomposition effectively, however, timber might not be easy to split down into pieces. Be aware that you'll require mixing the materials with Nitrogen-rich substances like we discussed earlier, because woody materials are abundant in Carbon but not Nitrogen!

Paper

It is crucial to think about the kind of paper you can recycle and which one you'll need to put in the recycling bin. There have been many complaints about the quality of ink that is used when creating the newspaper. What impact does this have on how compost is made? created? Since a while it was discovered that ink that was used in the past contained a number of chemicals, which are known to be hazardous.

With regard to the modern inks it is true that we can say that there have been significant improvements in the way that the majority of them are not harmful to use. However, not all types of papers can be composted. For instance, it is best to be wary of paper materials that have shiny advertisements, that are typically found in daily newspapers. Furthermore, even packaging of canned foods aren't free of chemical substances that could be more than the amount you'd like to compost. It has been proven that heavy metals like copper and zinc, when used in small quantities in pigments, can prove extremely beneficial and safe when composting. But, avoid ink pigments that are made of petroleum bases.

Although there are more and more questions about the use inks for printing on paper using paper, adding good suppliers to your compost heap could be the best options you'll ever make. Paper ads can assist in absorbing a lot of the water that is in the compost heap. This can prevent the growth of mold that can lead to unpleasant stinks. If you're experiencing too much of nitrogen-rich material in your compost it can help bring things back in balance with Carbon by deciding to include shredded paper. Since paper is a plant-based product and is a plant material, you'll be adding plants to the soil when you include it in your compost. In this way, you will aid in helping to "cure" soil that has already been depleted in nutrients.

It's not that difficult for you to make compost from paper. You can just dump huge pieces of paper in your compost bin and watch it decompose you think? Wrong! It is essential to be sure to shred your paper correctly so that it can break down enough. The paper must be turned into tiny pieces. Then, add them to your compost (the method you would use to add any other brown trash) and add a small bit of water, to help moisten the compost. Within a few months, you'll be able to make the perfect compost for your garden or even on your farm.

Straw

Straw is composed of the hollow stems that are left behind after you harvest wheat and grains. Straw can be useful for composting. Even though there are a few seeds within the straws, they will be okay and will not alter your compost in any negative way.

You can purchase straw from those who cultivate grains, even if you do not. Straw is stored in bales in order to appear neat. Bales may be round or square. The straw could have been laid on top of manure. Whatever type of straw you purchase it's great to compost. Straw is high in Carbon. Because it is dry, it can break when blended together with composting material. It can also serve as a foundation to add additional materials. Make sure to select straw harvested from a wholesome farm. There will be many advantages when you do this.

Pine Needles

Pine needles can make your bed appear very appealing. However, they are also recognized to be acidic and break down quite slowly. They're not as helpful as mulch for vegetable gardens because of their prickly characteristics until you completely compost them. Pine needles increase the amount of Carbon and boost the amount that you compost. They can be used to amend soil and mulch in a short amount of time. Let's talk about composting pine needles.

Utilizing a garden shredder, cut the pine needles into smaller pieces. Place a 2-inch layer of pine needles that have been shredded over the top of composting material (preferably green layers). Then, apply a half-inch layer manure over your pine needles. You can then add liquids to compost layer. If necessary, repeat the layering process until you reach an elevation of around 3 feet. It is essential to keep it damp. After that, you can make use of a pitch fork to turn the compost once every three days. If you observe the dark brown mass it means that your compost is prepared to be used. Because pine needles compost is already acidic it is not necessary to add line in soil unless a soil expert advises otherwise.

Sawdust to be used for composting

Sawdust is an "brown" materials for the composting process. This means it could be utilized to balance the Nitrogen-rich compost due to its carbon content. Sawdust is best added approximately 4:1 proportion with "green" material for composting. It's a good filler as it is able to absorb water quickly which is a great benefit to the process of composting.

The sawdust you get can be obtained from any kind of wood, soft or hard. But, avoid sawdust that comes from woods spray-painted with chemicals since certain chemicals can affect the process of composting. Making compost from sawdust is an incredible way to recover the value of the material that could have been wasted.

Nitrogen-rich Ingredients

Common sources of composting materials made from green and other ingredients are the kitchen waste, clippings of grass leaves, plant trimmings grass, livestock and vegan animal manure made by bats, pigs goats, cows, ducks and Pigeons. Other sources include all fruit and vegetable leftovers like salad scraps, the peels of bananas and melon rinds cores of apple and carrot peels. The manure of vegetarian animals is believed to be rich in nitrogen. The coffee grinds can also be highly recommended as they're rich in nitrogen.

How to Stock Your Organic Matter

It's essential to accumulate organic matter to compost. You'll require it to make the perfect compost pile. If you're just beginning it is possible that you don't have enough materials to build your compost pile in one sitting. That is you might not be able to complete a batch pile. You may have to add incrementally instead.

For starters begin, you should put your bin in close proximity to the compost bin. You could utilize circular bins constructed of chicken wire. It is recommended to connect scrap lumber or wooden pallets , together and make sure the bin is an easy access point and is covered. You can create a fantastic container from plastic sheet with holes that are extremely sturdy. It is possible to purchase the bin at the waste management office in your town close by, online or in the garden center.

Let's talk about the best method for making a stockpile of food scraps. In the beginning it is to empty food scraps that you have collected from your kitchen containers into a larger pail with a lid that is securely sealed. It is recommended to use a 5 gallon size as it is ideal to store your food in. To keep flies out it is recommended to put a few layers of newspaper inside the lid. Do not be worried about the liquid in the pail, as the food scraps that are decomposing can create the liquid. This is known as "compost tea". It is definitely delicious for the plant! It must be dumped to the trash bin. When you add new scraps of material in the container, you'll need sprinkle the surface of your waste with soil or compost already finished. The sawdust or rock dust, or peat moss may also be employed to eliminate odors and flies. When you realize that the pail is filled it is possible to make use of it to start the process of piling your batch. If you prefer, you could even decide to keep several of these pails with food scraps to last for a couple of weeks. Be sure to lock the lids. It is not recommended to put food scraps in the the top of a compost pile. Alwaysmake sure to put an inch or two of Brown material before you start.

Chapter 6: When To Begin Composting

The principle behind composting is to gather an assortment of biodegradable substances together, place them into a pile and then wait for them to disintegrate before they can be utilized. It's a simple concept but if you're trying to create the perfect level of compost to benefit your plants or enrich the soil, there has to be more more than this. This chapter will give you an in-depth look at composting and how you can take on the task.

The Carbon and Nitrogen Ratios. Carbon Ratio

In the preceding chapter, the compost components are split into carbon and strong nitrogen content. This is crucial since the mix of carbon and nitrogen makes for the non-smelly, fertile compost that is ideal for plants. According to research the ideal carbon-to- nitrogen ratio is 25-30:1. That means for one part of nitrogen there should be between 25 and 30 carbon parts. This ideal ratio will create the greatest quantity of heat, which allows the rapid break down of the organic matter. If there's excessive nitrogen, the compost begins to smell very unpleasant. Carbon in excess, however, will cause slow decomposition.

Selecting an Approach

As mentioned earlier there are a variety of options to choose according to what you're able to get. For composting at home there is the option of making use of a bin or your backyard soil to do the work. These are two of the most popular and practical options that are available. In this chapter, we will discuss the various options available for composting at home and the best way to get them to work.

Pit Composting

If you want to compost in a trench or pit choose a shaded space in your backyard, and preferably near the water. The pit is typically the ideal choice since it permits you to overly cover the area in order to improve the heat. The size and depth of the pit is contingent on the amount of compost you plan to create. The norm is that it should be at a minimum of one foot deep.

The fact that your compost is kept in an area that is not a good idea makes it difficult to get it out later to transfer it. Because of this, trench composting is the best option when you are planning of growing something over the soil. In this way, plants will instantly get nutrients through the soil, which will make into healthy and healthy.

Put all the organic material into the pit, making sure they're crushed to accelerate the process of composting. Remember the ratio above to ensure an acid and balanced nutrition for the soil and plants.

If you're still looking to fill the hole with organic matter you can try putting a small coating of organic brown soil over the top, then cover the hole with the Tarp. The brown layer contains carbon, which helps in warming the compost and at the same time keeping the smell from getting out.

After you're pleased with your compost, you can fill the pit by adding more soil. Continue this process until the pit is fully filled until the surface is completely covered prior to adding water to the soil over the pit. It's crucial to keep in mind that in areas with low oxygen levels underground, composting takes an extended time to complete. This is why keeping the area wet is the most effective way to stimulate the growth of bacteria. This can be done by ensuring that the soil surface is immersed in water at least a few times every week.

The great thing about this method is that it is easy to begin planting your seeds on top of the soil. However, underground compost needs all of a year to degrade. Therefore, you'll need to wait for a year before being permitted to plant anything over it and be sure it will flourish.

This type of composting pit can be described as the most simple, and requires little or no maintenance. It is ideal for those who don't have a lot of space to their backyards and don't wish to move the compost from one location to another.

Bin Composting

Certain homeowners might not have the land space to begin composting. It is also possible that you do not enjoy the smell or view of your house with the composting area just couple of feet away. To address this issue You can consider buying an organic compost bin that has locks that are solid to keep every biodegradable substance.

A garbage can is generally the best option for composting in bins. Before putting compost inside the container it should first be fitted with holes punched along the sides to allow aeration. Many people prefer to put up an upright pole with arms stationary within the center of their bin, to help blend the compost.

After having gathered all compost materials within this bin, then the upper portion is sealed and the organic matter remains to absorb heat and begin breaking down. The holes are designed to let the air flow inside while the pole performs the task of "turning" the pile in a way that the air is dispersed. This can be done by simply tumbling the entire bin several times with the inside pole assisting by mixing. If the bin is too large or too large, then doing it manually could be more efficient.

There are a variety of varieties of bins on the market that are specifically designed for composting. There's a rolling bin that is made to look like a ball with holes everywhere. A tumbler bin as well as covered bins also are in the market, which will aid in your decision.

Freestanding Compost

This is the most efficient method of getting you comfortable with the habit of composting. Freestanding composting means that you don't need to dig a hole or purchase an outdoor bin to begin the process. The ground that is bare is the primary site for compost. The way to do it:

Select a suitable location to compost the waste, preferring an area that is shaded and has enough room to move. Be sure to choose a location which is inundated and is only several steps away from the water faucet or water source.

Sprinkle brown materials on the ground, and use it as the base. Broken wood shavings or twigs will be ideal. Sprinkle water over this layer.

The next layer must have a brown color, however it must be it should be something that is more compact like brown leaves, paper or sawdust. Add about 4 inches before sprinkle water over the top.

Cover the pile with a cover and leave it as for the rest of the few days or. If you wish to accelerate the process of decomposition it is possible to turn the pile in order to introduce oxygen to the fragments that were compacted every week, prior to covering it with the tarp.

They are among the most commonly used and readily available options for homeowners to begin with composting. If you're thinking of using alternative methods described in the earlier chapters you can find additional details below.

Worm Composting

If you're not happy with the composting options provided above, you have the possibility of using worms for composting. This involves the use of insects to convert food waste into nutritious fertilizers for plants.

Find a container for worms where food scraps and worms will be mixed. It is necessary to have a specialized container for worms or follow the instructions for building one. Worm bins don't cost much and can be found through a variety of vendors.

Worms don't come in all shapes and sizes. To compost worms it is necessary to use the manure worm or red worm. These tiny critters eat on organic food , and make great fertilizers after eating food scraps. There are currently products made of worms that are available today, so you don't need to look for them.

Place some bedding in the bottom of your worm-catcher. Wet newspapers are ideal since the bedding has for it to become more liquid rather than hard. A few bits of wood chips may provide dust to the bedding which makes it ideal for worms. The bedding should cover about one-quarter from the container.

Set your container in an area that's the temperature of room. It is important not to let it become too hot or cold, because the worms would die or find the food scraps tasty.

The worm-to-food scraps proportion should not exceed 1 pounds to one pounds. The worm population increases quickly. In just two months your worm town of 30 may become 60! To avoid this, those who are new to composting worms are advised to begin by taking a step back and watch how their worms behave.

Place the worms in the bin by digging a hole into the center, then placing them inside and then filling the area with soil. It is then time to start putting in food scraps, and then increase the amount as you need. In time, your worm bin will be filled with fertilizers thanks to the worms. You can harvest this after your bedding is completely destroyed by the fertilizers.

The process of composting requires patience and effort. If you're new to composting techniques that are routine it may be better to avoid this first.

Chapter 7: The Basics Of Composting

If you've realized how valuable compost can be, you're likely to be eager to start in the process of composting. So let's talk about the process of making your own compost as well as the basic composting process. This is true regardless of whether you compost at home, on the allotment, or on small-scale farms.

First of all, a compost pile must always be started with bare soil as this will allow worms as well as others beneficial microorganisms rise out of the soil to be absorbed into your compost. This allows your compost to begin to break down and grow quicker. If you're composting off the surface or in membranes, then you can put in some shovels of soil as well as a few worms. I usually place any worms that I come across during weeding or digging into the compost pile since helps the compost break down.

Another one of my compost bins which is a bit wacky however very useful

It may not always be feasible to begin on the dirt however, if you are able to do it, then you should. If you're building compost bins using pallets, don't put an entire pallet on the base. Instead, you can utilize the pallets as a wall to wall off a portion of the soil, as seen in the image above.

The initial layer should consist of just a few inches of straw, or smaller twigs to aid in drainage and the aeration. Naturally, it would be in a perfect world and for the perfect compost pile, but the reality is that many people just dump things in because they don't possess straw at be found. If you spend the time to take this step, you'll see that your compost pile performs much better.

Compost is added in layers alternately adding moist components like food scraps, leaves, weeds, and dry materials like straw, leaves , and wooden Ash (in very thin layer). In reality, this will not be done precisely since it's not feasible when you're performing a lot of gardening, but if are able to arrange your compost into layers your compost will break down more quickly.

A lot of people keep plastic bags of compost full of straw or dry leaves specifically to layer their compost. If you are able to properly layer your compost the compost will decompose quicker and regular turning will be less crucial. When I throw on many weeds I also add a few handfuls of dried leaves or straw since this aids in aerating the compost. If you don't do this, it becomes an anaerobic soggy mass and there isn't enough oxygen to the bacteria responsible for the process of composting, and they end up dying! If you wish your compost to decay quickly then you must stack your compost and ensure that it is in aeration.

To begin the process of composting and to activate the pile you must include a nitrogen source like manure grass clippings, grass clippings or other green manure. I like to put in the wheelbarrow with freshly minted manure since it starts the process of composting. There are compost activators available However, you'll discover in the future if they are worth the money.

The process of composting requires water but not excessively otherwise it will stop as the bacteria that compost and insects get drowned. Let the rain do its work however, in dry weather it is possible provide your compost with a little water every time you turn it over to keep it moist. If it is rainy, you must protect your compost as if it becomes too moist the compost will cease to function. While some prefer carpet, I would recommend the use of tarpaulins since it's water resistant which means you can have some control on the quantity of water that is able to reach your compost.

The cover of your compost using carpet, cardboard or sheets will help keep heat and moisture within, which speed up the process of breaking down the material. It also helps prevent the compost from becoming excessively wet. Another advantage of covers is that they will help to keep vermin away. A well-groomed compost is not a victim of rodents or mice.

However, when you do discover they are in your compost it is important to make sure you keep them out. The warmness of a compost pile may draw all kinds of animals from rodents to snakes to hedgehogs that want to hide to keep warm. Be sure to check your compost pile to see if there are signs of animals in it and, should it appear as if it hasbeen there, be wary when pouring it over.

Rotating your compost once every two to three weeks will keep your compost aerated. This allows the bacteria to gain the oxygen they require to breakdown the material that is discarded. If you don't turn the compost regularly, it will turn into a sloppy mass of weeds , which lacks oxygen for good bacteria live. Even if you've added lots of straw, it's nevertheless worth turning your compost with pitchforks or a shovel to ensure there's enough oxygen. To ensure that your compost is breaking down quickly, you need to turn it each week and add some manure in order to keep the bacterial levels at a high.

If you don't turn your compost for some time or it is very wet and muddy, then you should dig it up with manure in order to begin the composting process when you turn it. The bacteria responsible for composting needs oxygen, as does all living things. When your compost becomes excessively wet the air pockets that are forming between the compost material break down, removing oxygen out of the system. This is why the beneficial bacteria die and the compost becomes damp and smelly. A little manure or garden soil can revive the process, but.

If your compost bins have been in place, it's recommended to add more materials by mixing them in instead of adding it to the top. This will help keep it aerated and speed up the process of composting. After a successful weeding session, I like to get the plants in a little then add some manure, afterwards cover with straw.

It is possible to purchase composters or create yourself composting bins it's up to you and budget. More on both options later. Consider purchasing an compost tumbler. It helps in turning the process however, you're restricted in the amount of compost you can put into one. They generally work well for small gardens and those who do not generate much compostable material.

The Carbon Ratio of Nitrogen / Carbon

The material you include to your compost pile is either nitrogen or carbon-based in different amounts depending on the type of material. To make your compost pile perform efficiently, you must to ensure that there is a balance between the two components. Be assured that it's not nearly as complicated as it sounds and doesn't require a degree in chemistry.

Carbon-rich materials include dry things like tiny branches of vegetable peelings, plant stems as well as sawdust, wood chip corn stalks, dried leaves coffee filters as well as paper bags that have been shredded straw, egg shells peat moss, wood ash as well as conifer needles. They make your compost have a light and fluffy appearance. They are often called brown materials.

Nitrogen is present in protein-rich materials, generally moist, like food scraps and green lawn clippings. It is also found in manures, and green leaves. These are the basic substances used to produce composting enzymes. They are commonly referred to as green materials since they are, generally green in color.

They can be a bit confused mix of the two due to the green leaves that are nitrogen-rich and the plant stems that are carbon-rich. There is no need to divide the weeds into leaves and stems You can simply place them in your compost pile, and then include more carbon-rich (brown) substances.

To ensure that your compost pile will be healthy, you require more carbon-rich materials as opposed to nitrogen-rich ones. In general that you should add one-third of green material to 2/3 brown. In reality, this might not be practical since after a thorough weeding session, you'll have a amount of nitrogen-rich material. In these instances you must get the compost out and then add some brown matter whenever you can. If you rotate your pile slightly every day for about a week after adding the newly added material, you will prevent the extra green matter from that is clogging your compost and kill the beneficial bacteria.

The brown matter adds bulk to your compost pile , allowing oxygen flow into it's middle to nourish the beneficial bacteria and organisms that live the pile. A lot of nitrogen-rich material (green) will result in an unpleasant, smelly heap of plant matter that is rotting and is slowly decomposing because it is now anaerobic. Typically, you cover the fresh nitrogen rich materials with carbon-rich material that hides the stink and keeps the composting process in motion.

Composting with No-Turn

It is believed to be the most unpleasant component of composting since it can be a lot of work and smell a bit. If you find bugs living in your compost This is the time you get them disturbed and they fly through the air and can be a bit dangerous for all. There are also bugs and other bugs who have settled within your pile of compost. We'll go over the advantages and disadvantages of turning compost in the near future however for now, I'll show you how to construct an organic compost pile that does not require turning.

When you are building your compost pile, make sure that you add lots of coarse materials such as straw. If you have straw (which isn't costly) close to the compost, then you can add straw each time you add new green material. This will help your compost disintegrate quickly, almost as fast as the time it would take to turn it. The resulting compost will contain a higher amount of nitrogen.

A compost pile that is not turned over is typically created in a compost container in which you add fresh material to the top , and then remove the final product from the bottom, like"dalek", a black, plastic containers commonly utilized by gardeners. Making compost inside a compost bin is a challenge, which is why this technique will make your compost bin more efficient and useful for you in speeding the process of composting.

What do you do with all That Leaves

Incorporating some leaves into your compost pile is beneficial to do However, the addition of too many leaves isn't. It is possible to get rid of too many leaves, especially if have a lot of trees in your yard and take a lengthy time to fully break down. The extra leaves can be turned into its compost pile in a shaded area and with drainage that is appropriate. We'll talk more about the process of making leaf mould later in the book, as it is extremely beneficial for your garden. But, since leaves take longer to breakdown it is not the most ideal choice for your compost pile since they will not be been completely composted when you need to utilize the compost.

It is possible to make a leaf-mould tea by wrapping leaves in burlap and placing it in the water in a bucket to stay for 3 days. Then, take the leaves out and place the leaves in your compost and utilize the water to make an liquid fertiliser.

Compost Bins that are enclosed Bins

If you are looking for compost with smaller amounts the container that is enclosed is more practical since they keep the waste from view and out of reach. You can build your own out of a bin that is heavy-duty by drilling half-inch holes for aeration around the can every 6 to 8 inches around the container. If you are adding new materials mix it all up to make sure it's properly Aerated.

The brick prevents the lid from falling off and assists in weighing down the bin.

There are compost bins made of plastic with an upper lid and an opening in the bottom that has the option of sliding doors. They are the most popular composting containers for homes and are relatively inexpensive to purchase. The only drawback is that they can be hard to make the compost turn however, you can purchase the right tool to do this. They can take longer to produce your compost, however they are perfect for a smaller garden that does not require lots of compost in a short time. It is also not a lot of work involved in creating composting areas as well as they are relatively simple to move, even if full. All you have to do is raise them, move them, and after that, move your compost that also turns it.

Compost tumblers are ideal for small amounts of compostable material. They're also very simple to turn and utilize. If you struggle to turn their compost pile they are the perfect. A tumbler speedily speeds the process of composting and can be used all year in addition to preventing pests infiltrating your compost. The disadvantage is that they are small in comparison to compost piles you can construct yourself, but is still an option for many for a variety of reasons, including to enhance bigger compost bins or for those with an area that is smaller. It's worth having one of these as compost piles as the compost that is made in tumblers breaks down more quickly since it is frequently turned. You can make use of a compost tumbler in order to make compost while your primary compost pile works in a slower manner.

One of the biggest distinctions when composting using tumblers is that they generally fill it in one go and not add compostable material a little at a given time as you do in the other bins for compost. This is due to the fact that with many tumblers, you are unable to remove just a tiny amount of compost at a given time, but you must remove all of it at once.

Chapter 8: Making A Compost Heap

The process of making a compost pile is not difficult and there are plenty of ways to tackle this. It all depends on your space, budget and time to decide what is best for you.

Perhaps the most well-known type that composting can be found in is the basic (usually) charcoal composter.

They can be found in many garden stores and are affordable to buy. They're not the most efficient method to make compost as you'll discover while going through the article, but they're the most convenient. Compost can take a bit longer in these because of the absence of circulation and air flow yet it happens.

The best feature of compost containers is they are placed at an ideal angle in your garden, and conceal the compost from view and secure it. They have an easy-access door in the front for access to your compost when it's done, but be careful with these doors since they tend to be flimsy and easily break off.

There are some city councils that will offer the bins at an affordable price to decrease the amount of garbage they will have to take away from you. If your city has this option, it's worthwhile to take advantage of the offer as it will help you save money as well as is an easy way to begin composting.

They aren't the largest compost bins, and that you're unable to fill it very quickly, especially when you attempt to place garden waste inside and kitchen waste in. The majority of people who utilize these bins usually use two or three bins to deal with the amount of waste they generate and the compost they produce.

Be sure the surface that you place them on is level. Otherwise, you could see the compost leaked out from the bottom or even rodents are able to get into the compost bin to eat kitchen garbage.

Another kind of compost bin that is most definitely the best is the big compost bin made of wood.

You can purchase them ready put together or make them out of pallets made from wood. Many delivery and manufacturing companies get their products on pallets, and are eager to dispose of the pallets that are not being used. A quick trip around an industrial zone will show many companies that utilize pallets, and many will provide some for free if you come to their offices and ask.

Most often, those who are dedicated to composting will usually have three or four of them next to one next to each. This is to ensure they can make compost with ease, which you'll learn more about in the future.

If you're making your own composter out of wood, it is essential to ensure that the front is movable as it will make access to the compost much simpler. It is possible to make the compost bins tri-sided If you like, however there is a chance of having pets or children inside the compost container and creating an obnoxious mess.

A carpeted piece or plastic sheeting can be utilized to cover this kind of compost pile. Make sure to put it in a weighing container with rocks so that it doesn't slough off at any time.

This type of compost heap is extremely beneficial since the wood is an excellent insulation to keep the heat in , ensuring that compost can be created. The spaces between the wooden blanks allow air to circulate turn around and allow you to access the compost to rake it or rotate it frequently.

If you construct one of these using pallets, then the price will be low. You can also purchase them in kits on the internet as well as from garden stores, and they're usually slightly less expensive than plastic bins you see above.

They're by far the most effective method of composting and, if you've got enough space having three or four will guarantee you have a an ongoing supply of high-quality compost for your garden.

There's a middle ground between these two types of composting. It is the composter that is tumbler.

This type of composter has a limited space, but it can produce compost extremely quickly. It is all you have to do is place your garbage into it and at least once a week you pull a handle from the side to turn it around. The compost is mixed and accelerates the process.

This is the most efficient method to make compost, but you will have to fight to make space, and it could be quite challenging to take the humus out of the composter, rather than the kitchen scraps that aren't gone to compost.

They are the most costly compost bins available and can be purchased on the internet or at the local garden shop. While they cost more however, they are a lot more effective in making compost.

It's beautiful and does not take up a lot of space. It is ideal for people with a smaller yard who doesn't want to have a large compost bin that blocks the views.

There are three primary compost bin types can be found, even though there are many varieties of them available in the market. They all have the same purpose.

At the conclusion of the day the type of compost bin will lead to:

Your budget

Your available space

How gorgeous you'd like to appear

Whatever one you pick, you might want to purchase something similar for your kitchen , so you can easily place your compost in a container before you take it out into the composter.

Another option one thing that many appreciate is buying compostable plastic bags that you can put in your compost bins indoors that keep it tidy and makes transporting compost outdoors very simple.

As you will see, composting doesn't require much money and can be accomplished efficiently and quickly.

What Should You Put in Your Compost Heap

This is an essential section because you must ensure that you are putting the correct things in your compost pile at home. Don't put the right things in and it could be too slow to break them down or, more seriously you may end up planting your garden with weeds!

The most typical thing you'll put in the kitchen is food scraps that have been discarded from your meals. It is crucial that you don't place anything that has been cooked in your compost bin as this could draw rodents. You should only place raw vegetables and fruits into your compost pile.

Peelings of carrots and potatoes are perfect for composting in a bin , as are any leftover fruits or pieces of vegetables. Don't put peaches, stones, plums and other food items in there as they will not be able to break down and you may result in unwanted trees within your yard.

Eggshells can also be incorporated and tea bags in your compost, as they can give nutrients to the soil. If you prepare fresh coffee using coffee beans, then the grinds that are used could be placed into your compost pile. It is also possible to use them in the same way as the best compost for growing mushrooms in.

If you're storing your compost inside the house prior to transferring it to your compost pile Don't leave it for too long before removing it. If you let it sit long enough, the compost will begin to smell, rot and draw insects. Be aware of the size of the bin that you store your compost because If it's too big you could fill up the compost bin, and it may weigh too much to carry out and then tip over into the compost heap.

Kitchen garbage is the most widely used material that is used in compost piles, however when you use only this then your compost pile gets moist and draws insects.

To prevent this from happening, you have to add the cut grass or leaf litter each time. This will prevent the compost from becoming a breeding ground for flies and becoming too wet.

Garden waste is the second item you'll put into your compost pile and it is important to ensure that what you throw in will be broken down in an acceptable amount of period of. The idea of putting sticks or huge stalks of wood from plants in your compost is an unnecessary waste of time since it'll take way too long to break them down. When you are ready to take out your beautiful brown humus, only to discover it's full of pieces of sticks as well as other bits which you must remove before it is able to be utilized.

They must be put out to be collected by the municipal garbage collectors. This kind of thing is going to take a long time to breakdown, and will affect how well your compost is able to be used.

You can utilize grass cuttings, leaves and plants from your garden to your compost pile. They're extremely beneficial because they can help stop your compost pile from becoming too wet. They also aid in keeping it warm to ensure that the process of composting can occur.

However, it is important to be aware when adding weeds as you're trying to avoid the introduction of harmful weeds into your compost. If you do this, then you run the risk that they'll remain in the compost for a while and grow back after spreading the compost all over your garden.

For instance, dandelion leafs are fine to add to your compost pile, however, don't put the flowers or the roots into it. The seeds of the flowers may sprout when you spread your compost, especially if the compost isn't hot enough. Dandelions can develop from a single portion of root, therefore when you cut off the root of a dandelions, then several dandelions could grow from it.

The same is true for the nettles. Don't hesitate to place the nettle stalks into the compost. They are great for compost, however, don't include the roots.

Be aware of which weeds are harmful and which ones aren't. Normal grass, like is able to go in your compost pile, but cooch grass can't go in your compost since it can regenerate from the root.

If you own any plants that have leaves that are suffering from diseases, then you must not put them into your compost pile because it could cause the disease to spread when you make use of your compost. If your potatoes are suffering from Blight, you can't add them to your compost pile. If the leaves on your roses are becoming black, then they also cannot be put in your compost bin.

There is no need to add any animal carcasses in your compost, as it isn't able to be broken down and will draw rodents and other scavengers that is probably not something you want to have in your garden.

Don't put pet or cat garbage in the compost container because it isn't able to be able to break down and could transmit the toxocara virus throughout the compost and onto your plants. It may also contain roundworms or tapeworms which could infect you or your family members via the plants that live in your compost.

It is important to take your time going through your weeds to ensure you can put the correct kinds in the compost pile. But, it can decrease the amount of trash that has to be cleared from your home.

If you're cautious about the things you add to your compost pile and ensure that you keep harmful big sticks and weeds in your garden, you'll discover that you can make incredible compost in a matter of minutes.

Composting Chemistry: The Chemistry of Composting

While a thorough discussion of chemistry isn't required to start composting, having an understanding of the process as well as the composition of compost can assist you in making it more efficient. If you understand the process, it is possible to assure that you'll make the highest quality compost that you can.

Nitrogen is a vital chemical you should include in your soil, and many plants rely on nitrogen for their growth. Food scraps, manure that is well-rotted as well as grass cuttings and weeds all contribute nitrogen to your compost.

Carbon is also vital to your compost and your plans , and this is made up of woody twigs and chippings straw, sawdust, straw newspaper, and brown leaves. cardboard. In the event that your compost is becoming wet and you don't have access to leaves or grass cuttings, you can scrunch newspaper or cut pieces of cardboard and place it in your compost.

Also, in winter when you're not cutting the grass, and the trees aren't shed with leaves, add newspapers or even cardboard (the brown material, not the glossy printed material) in your compost to ensure that the balance is in the right direction.

As a rule of the thumb, if something is green and/or sappy , it will create nitrogen. However, the case of dry, woody or brown, it will produce carbon.

To get the most compost, you're looking for two parts nitrogen and one part carbon. This means that you will require about twice as much as the green material in your compost as the brown woody material.

They work in tandem to create the most effective compost. The carbon traps air inside the compost. This assists the bacteria do their work and break down the waste into usable humus.

There are those who argue that it is necessary to use ingredients in your compost, however when you're managing it well, then there's no reason to add them. An activator for compost is just a fantastic source of nitrogen, therefore when you're putting a lot of nitrogen-rich materials in your compost, you don't need an activator. A well-made compost heap will produce the required microorganisms by itself and you can aid by mixing the compost pile.

If you're looking to add an additive, one of the most effective and least expensive alternatives is urine from humans, as it is very high in nitrogen. However, how you incorporate it into your compost bin is dependent on you.

The most efficient way to create compost, and it is the most efficient for most of us because it takes the least amount of time to add your garbage items into your compost bin in a cyclical manner (in 2 parts nitrogen to 1 carbon proportion) to ensure that the container is filled and fully settled. It is then possible to add your waste items into the upper part of your bin, and the compost will rise out from the bottom. It is easy to fill up a compost bin and you should keep a few in order you will keep a steady source of compost.

If you have open compost containers, or have lots of waste produced in a single time, the fastest method is to stack all of your compost in an orderly pile. After a week, turn the pile over and following a second week, you can turn it back. Then , cover the pile in black plastic sheeting, and then cover it with it. In three or four months, you'll have compost that is ready to use!

It's possible to do this in the compost bin, however it's easier to do this to use an open composter since you can rotate the pile more easily.

Heating is vital for compost piles and you must ensure that the compost heap is properly insulated. This is why the majority of compost bins are made of black, and we utilize black plastic sheets, which aids in keeping heat in the heap, and that's an area where it has positive effects.

Typically, the temperature between 55 to 70°F, the bacteria known as psychrophiles begin to grow. When the temperature rises above 70, and eventually to 90, mesophiles begin to appear and they consume everything and raise the temperature to 100 F. When temperatures reach 100F the mesophiles die.

The thermophiles at temperatures over 90F do an amazing job. They last between three to five days, and while they work, the compost pile gets hot, and it's almost too hot! This is a good thing as this will kill off the seeds and weeds within your compost. If your compost isn't at this temperature , there's the likelihood that you won't get rid of them and end up spreading them throughout your garden.

It is at this point when you must rotate your compost pile as it lets more air into it and gives you an even more nutritious mix. When the compost heap is cooling and the woodlice, worms and other insects are able to help to reduce the amount of compost more. A lot of gardeners search for worms in their gardens and then put them into the compost pile to aid in this process.

So, that's your compost's science lesson, straightforward isn't it? If you can remember this and make sure you have the mix of nitrogen and carbon perfect to make your own compost you'll be able to make excellent compost that will aid your plants to grow.

Compost Actuators

There are some who advise you to make use of an activator for your compost. It isn't needed if you've got the proper proportion of materials, since the compost pile will heat up naturally in its own time.

But there are many compost piles that are properly balanced and have enough nitrogen and carbon. In winter, it is often difficult to put the grass clippings and leaves to the compost bin. Then you are forced to fill it up with kitchen waste and newspapers.

If you're accumulating an excessive amount of brown material, and not enough green, nitrogen-rich material that is inside your composter,, then you'll need an activator. The nitrogen creates an ignition source to warm the entire compost bin.

You might find you are mild , and once the temperature drops below 50F or 12C then the process of composting slows down and ceases. If you must do this during spring time, you might need to add an activator to kick it off.

Chapter 9: Simple Compost Creation Process

To better comprehend the process of making compost, you can test an easy method that is described below. This is the most basic kind of compost that can be utilized in your garden or lawn. If you're using only a few ingredients, it can take a while in order for your compost to be prepared. Therefore, let's start the process.

For the beginning of compost creation , you should have an existing compost bin. If you don't have a compost container, you could choose a patch of land for your own compost. It is possible to protect the land with the Tarp. Or, you can purchase compost bins which are extremely simple to utilize. All you need to do is put in the garbage and then close the lid.

At first, you must fill the area of land with waste from plants. This could include things like dried leaves, dead weeds Dead leaves, dead twigs grass clippings dried flowers and remnants of fruit. Also, you can add leftovers in your home. This could be vegetable or fruit waste, eggshellsand seeds and so on. If there are birds at your house, you could include bird excrement to your compost pile. Also, don't forget to add the dried grass that you have gathered off your yard. Mix all of these ingredients using spading fork. Add some soil to your compost. Then cover the area of the land with the sheet of tarp. If you're using a composting bin, it is best to simply close the lid.

* In the course of a few days, you can include more vegetable and plant waste to your compost. Additionally, you can sprinkle the compost using water. This will speed up the process of decomposition.

* After 3-4 months, you are able to check for compost. Stir it using a spading fork.

* Sprinkle water on the initial layer of compost. Water is vital for the proper decomposition of all material waste. Sprinkle some soil over the compost and mix everything using spading fork. If the compost's bottom has become spongy and brown, this indicates that your compost is

ready to use. Mix it well before spreading the compost over your garden.

* Use a shovel to mix compost and soil. Remove some soil from near the plant's roots. Mix the compost together and fill the area with soil. Also , sprinkle some water.

* You can make use of this compost several times. You can begin to prepare more compost to ensure it is prepared by the time you've finished your current supply of compost.

If you're planning to compost your garden There are many choices available to you. In the first place, you should choose a medium-sized compost bin that will ensure that your compost is available at the time you require it. If you're using an enormous compost bin the compost will require longer to decompose. This is due to the fact that you will be adding more waste and other waste into the compost. For example, if you're running a composting bin that is about 1 m in cube, it could hold plenty of garbage. As debris begins to break down, they are converted to Humus. The process can reduce the volume of waste. This will leave room for you to include additional organic material. Therefore, it is recommended to get a moderate size compost bin. There are two or three bins. Within 3-4 months, your compost will be in good shape. When your first compost pile is ready, you can begin filling your additional compost containers.

This will help to have a steady amount of compost in your garden.

Tips To Compost Creation

* The length of time needed to create compost depends on many factors including the components you include in the bin for compost.

* Climate is a crucial aspect that can affect the process of compost creation. The process of composting in summer is quicker. Warmer weather promotes the development of microorganisms and microorganisms. Naturally, the process of decomposition accelerates when the surrounding is warmer.

Moisture is an essential ingredient that influences the development of compost that is rich. Insufficient moisture can slow down degradation as well as the growth of bacteria. This is why farmers frequently spray water over their composting bins. But, too much water could harm the compost. The compost must be moist but not damp. In excess watering, you can harm the process of forming humus. Therefore, it is important to be extra cautious when adding water to your compost. It is recommended to employ a water sprayer order to bring water into your compost. This will ensure that the water is evenly spread. The compost should be stirred when you add water.

This will allow the compost to mix with water and turn wet and rich.

As previously mentioned the items you put to your compost bin can affect the process of making compost. If you are adding more solid plant wastes such as branches and twigs, the process of decay may take longer than you expected. Twigs and branches made of wood are not able to decompose quickly. If you're in need of a fertilizer that is quick, don't add excessive twigs and branches. Also, you can add more sappy items such as vegetables such as dried flowers, rotten leaves as well as food wastes that are rotten.

Instead of spreading plain water, you could use the waste water in your kitchen. For instance, the water from the dishwashing of your grains and vegetables could be used to moisten the bin for compost. The water is rich in nutrients, and therefore it can speed up the process of creating compost.

The amount of items you put in the compost bin will also impact the speed at which compost is created. If you include large chunks of wood, twigs, and other cut vegetable matter to compost, they could take longer to break down. So, if you're trying to get some compost in the ground quickly, then you should reduce the size of the material. Reduce the twigs, twigs, and veggies into smaller pieces and then put them into your compost pile.

* If you plan to make use of your compost within 3 months, do not add items like egg

shells. These substances are high in nutrients, but take a some time to break down. If you are planning to add these substances, then you will have to wait six months before you can see the items broken down in organic matter.

* If you plan to sell your compost then adhere to the guidelines set by Soil Association. Therefore, you should not restrict certain products and must also limit the time of the composting process.

* If the weather has been warm or moderate and your compost creation will be finished in approximately three months. However, if the climate is cold, then wait for another three months.

To ensure that your compost pile is decomposing at a satisfactory rate, you should monitor the heap on a regular basis. This will enable you take appropriate steps to enhance the process of compost creation. If, for instance it seems that there is a deficiency of moisture, you can sprinkle some water on. If it appears to be quite damp, you could remove the lid or covering and let the air dry out any water residue that has accumulated.

When you are filling up your compost pile, you must include easily decomposable material toward the top and move all the tough things to the bottom layer. This will help even help in the process of composting.

Note that the production of heat is one of the main indicators that reveal the process of compost creation. In the process of decomposition, it releases heat as an byproduct. Most likely, this will occur in the first month. Be cautious when you lift the bin's lid. If the heat production is high, it could emit hot vapours.

* If the source of heat is located on the upper side then your compost should be done in about 2 to three months. If it is on the lower part this could be a little longer.

* Following the initial stage of heat production, there is cooling phase. In this stage, you may add more manure or debris. In this phase, you can also make the compost turn. The process of turning is one in which the entire pile made of

compost can be turned upside-down. This helps make it easier to even out the process of decay throughout the heap. Debris along the edges that remain unaffected must be moved onto the middle, and reverse.

* It does not have to be necessary every time you turn compost around. If you think that the decomposition process is quick, then do not change it. Simply stir it up with a spading fork , and let it sit for about a week. Be sure to check your compost every week and continue stirring until it's all at the point of being ready.

* If you're making use of a closed plastic container the compost will get ready earlier. If you're using an open bin or any

container at all, the process could take longer.

Along with the regular water sprays, you should also add a little dirt to the compost pile. This will assist you to create a more nutritious compost.

When the compost is in place, you can put it in the soil. Get rid of all the strange branches, twigs and other pieces that aren't fully decomposed. When adding compost, you must remove the upper layer of soil and spread the compost out evenly. Mix it in with soil, then cover it off with another top layer. Sprinkle water on the entire area and let it remain in peace.

Do not add meat products , animal or human excrement to your compost. This could attract pests as well as animals. This can also encourage the growth of weeds.

Conclusion

It is easy to compost and extremely cost-effective. In the current times living, this need of the time has become feasible. A billion dollars are spent each year for garbage collection fertilizer production, garbage collection, and environmental cleanup. Although some of these can be avoided There are numerous ways to reduce your gardening costs and help the environment.

This Book is a user-friendly composting guide to get started. Beginning today you'll observe these newspaper and other fruits and vegetables in different ways.

You know what they mean when they say"One person's trash is another's treasure, and the trash in your home could turn into black gold if it is allowed to it.

Now, you've got every trick, recipe, and suggestions; let's start by composting!

www.ingramcontent.com/pod-product-compliance
Lightning Source LLC
Chambersburg PA
CBHW071836080526
44589CB00012B/1014